I Can Be Anything!

I CAN BE A PILOT

By Miller Slenzak

Please visit our website, www.garethstevens.com. For a free color catalog of all our high-quality books, call toll free 1-800-542-2595 or fax 1-877-542-2596.

Cataloging-in-Publication Data

Names: Slenzak, Miller.
Title: I can be a pilot / Miller Slenzak.
Description: New York : Gareth Stevens Publishing, 2019. | Series: I can be anything! | Includes index.
Identifiers: LCCN ISBN 9781538217665 (pbk.) | ISBN 9781538217641 (library bound) | ISBN 9781538217672 (6 pack)
Subjects: LCSH: Air pilots–Juvenile literature. | Airplanes–Piloting–Vocational guidance–Juvenile literature.
Classification: LCC TL547.S48 2019 | DDC 387.7092–dc23

First Edition

Published in 2019 by
Gareth Stevens Publishing
111 East 14th Street, Suite 349
New York, NY 10003

Editor: Kate Mikoley
Designer: Laura Bowen

Photo credits: Cover, p. 1 (kid) glenda/Shutterstock.com; cover, p.1 (background) Andrey Khachatryan/Shutterstock.com; pp. 5, 24 pio3/Shutterstock.com; p. 7 Who is Danny/Shutterstock.com; p. 9 Benny Marty/Shutterstock.com; pp. 11, 24 Alexey Y. Petrov/Shutterstock.com; p. 13 Atosan/Shutterstock.com; pp. 15, 24 Carolyn Franks/Shutterstock.com; p. 17 Zdorov Kirill Vladimirovich/Shutterstock.com; p. 19 Marina Zezelina/Shutterstock.com; p. 21 Digital Vision/Photodisc/Getty Images, p. 23 Hero Images/Getty Images.

Printed in the United States of America

CPSIA compliance information: Batch #CS18GS: For further information contact Gareth Stevens, New York, New York at 1-800-542-2595.

Contents

Pilots fly planes!
Some fly helicopters.

They fly around
the world.

Some fly over the sea!

BOSE
VH-ZVD
R44 Clipper II

Pilots sit in the cockpit. This is at the front of the plane.

They use controls.
These help the plane go.

FUEL CONTROL
RUN
CUTOFF
STAB
NORM
CUTOUT
AUTOBRAKE
PARKING BRAKE PULL
NOSE UP
FLAP
VHF
ACTIVE
STBY-1/2
<121.200←L→130.955>
<DATA - C - 126.200>
<121.500 - R - 133.300>
<STORE ACTIVE

Pilots land at an airport.

1863
FLAMMABLE
JET A

Some fly small planes.

Others fly big planes.
I went on a big plane!

This is Ms. Brady.
She flew the plane
to Florida.

I can be a pilot.
So can you!

Words to Know

airport

cockpit

helicopter

Index